MIDTOWN AND UPTOWN MANHATTAN AERIALS
THROUGH TIME

RICHARD PANCHYK

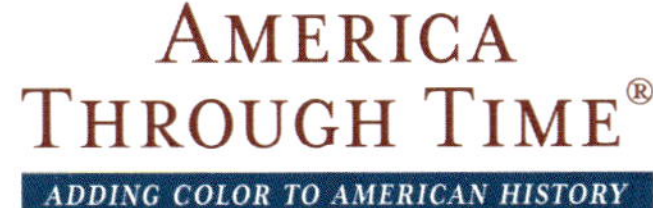

Acknowledgments

Thank you, as always, to Alan Sutton and Kena Longabaugh for their unwavering support of my mission to document local history in photographs.

Image Credits
Library of Congress: 4–10, 14, 23, 55 bottom, 57–68, 69 top, 74, and 89
National Archives: 11–13, 15–22, 24–54, 55 top, 56, 70, 71 top, and 77–78
USGS: 76
Matthew Panchyk: 92
All other images courtesy of the author.

America Through Time is an imprint of Fonthill Media LLC
www.through-time.com
office@through-time.com

Published by Arcadia Publishing by arrangement with Fonthill Media LLC
For all general information, please contact Arcadia Publishing:
Telephone: 843-853-2070
Fax: 843-853-0044
E-mail: sales@arcadiapublishing.com
For customer service and orders:
Toll-Free 1-888-313-2665

www.arcadiapublishing.com

First published 2022

Typeset in Mrs Eaves XL Serif Narrow
Printed and bound in England

Introduction

Distance lends enchantment to the view.
Mark Twain

The aerial photograph is a direct descendant of the bird's-eye view or panoramic map, which was essentially a detailed (often in color) drawing of a place from a high vantage point. For centuries, the only way to "see" the entirety of a place in one glance was through these views, which were especially popular in the nineteenth and early twentieth centuries. In the United States, they were expressions of hometown pride and also fired the public imagination about more exotic locales elsewhere in the country.

The nineteenth century in America was one of major growth and change; these bird's-eye views showed the impressive size of everything from small towns to major cities such as New York. They were usually drawn to represent the view from 2,000 to 3,000 feet, but they were generally not drawn to scale. They were often created in full color for added visual impact. Of course, some bird's-eye views could simply be taken from places where there was a hill or high vantage point that could be used for sketching the view below. For locations where that was not an option (such as nineteenth-century New York City), an accurate bird's-eye view could only be created by taking street-level information and carefully plotting it as if seen from an overhead perspective. There were a few prolific bird's-eye view artists in the country; some 55 percent of the more than 1,700 panoramic maps in the collections of the Library of Congress were created by just five artists.

The bird's-eye view on the next page was published in the 1880s. In the nineteenth-century world depicted here, the tallest points in the city were church steeples, the towers of the Brooklyn Bridge, and the masts of the ships in the harbor. And since almost nobody had access to church steeples or ship's masts, there was really no other way to "view" the city from above besides bird's-eye views such as this. Aside from the historical and sentimental value of the image, the general small size and uniformity of much of the city's buildings make this image less interesting than the aerial photographs taken when the city and its buildings were larger.

The earliest aerial photograph was taken by a Frenchman from a hot air balloon in 1858, but the art of aerial photography did not really have a chance to "take off" until the advent of the airplane. The earliest aerial photographic views of Midtown Manhattan locales were often the ones taken from atop newly built skyscrapers, which were the highest points for miles around (a few such images are included in this book). The earliest airplanes did not offer ideal conditions for the taking of photographs, but by the late 1910s, high quality aerial images could be snapped from planes.

Many of the vintage aerial views in this book were taken by military photographers, and thus precise information about dates, times, and altitudes was recorded. By 1923, there were fifteen

Bird's-eye view of New York City in the 1880s.

photographic sections of the United States Army Air Service in the country, and two of them were attached to Mitchel Field on Long Island—the 8th and the 14th. The original photographs can be quite valuable; in 2018, an archive of fifty-seven original Mitchel Field army aerial photographs dating to between 1923 and 1925 was offered for sale by a rare book dealer for $7,500. But military planes were not the only conduits for aerial views; the largest commercial aerial photographer was Fairchild Aerial Surveys, which was founded in 1924 by Sherman Mills Fairchild.

The altitudes of the aerial images in this book range mainly from 600 to 23,000 feet. It is interesting to see how altitude and angle can have a major impact on the way we perceive Manhattan. The lowest altitude images give you the amazing yet eerie feeling of being eye-level with the tops of the skyscrapers of the day while the highest altitude photos seem to capture New York as a highly detailed impossibly small-scale diorama of the kind you can see at the Queens Museum in Flushing Meadow Corona Park.

Aside from photographs taken from airplanes, many of the images in this book were taken from the windows or roofs of other buildings high enough to offer an "aerial" perspective on New York City, and from other elevated vantage points such as the High Line. Today's drone technology allows for a new and exciting way for the average person to get aerial views of places—but not New York City, where regulations largely prohibit the use of drones.

Mid-twentieth century aerial views of Manhattan had the potential for mass appeal and quickly wound up on postcards—the perfect, affordable way to capture the essence of this inspiring place with one image that features all or most of the points of interest. Some of the most popular Midtown and Uptown postcard aerial views over the last several decades show the Empire State Building and the Chrysler Building—from an aerial perspective that can offer a view of the buildings that cannot be had from ground level.

Looking at aerial photographs over the years can tell us a lot about ourselves and our neighborhoods, about urban development and aesthetics. They are great snapshots of New York City

Looking south from the Met Life Building in 1912.

history and of architectural styles and urban planning norms of the time. Some aerial views of Midtown Manhattan are especially revealing about New York as a port city; the docks and wharves are numerous and impressive, and the marine traffic is heavy. In the 1920s, one oceangoing steamer entered the port, and one left every twenty minutes during daytime hours. In 1929 alone, 6,928 vessels engaged in foreign trade entered the Port of New York. In 1929, the value of import and export goods entering and leaving New York was over $4 billion and weighed almost 27 billion tons. Every conceivable product was received and shipped from New York in great quantities. As of 1930, there were thirty-eight warehouses in New York City just for the storage of tea.

The other aspect of Midtown Manhattan that comes across quite loudly in these images is how the cluster of skyscrapers began in the central area between roughly Lexington Avenue and Sixth Avenue from 34th to 50th Streets and spread outward from there. Many of the photographs of Midtown coincide with the construction of the Chrysler Building and Empire State Building in early 1930s. As for Uptown Manhattan, improvements such as Riverside Park, the Henry Hudson Parkway, and the George Washington Bridge all changed the landscape forever.

These photos, many of them previously unpublished, are fun to study. Maybe you will find something surprising upon closer inspection. It is the little details that are the most fascinating, like the wisps of steam coming from ships, the changing signs in Times Square, the architectural details of some long-gone building, or the difference in the Empire State Building pre- and post- television antenna. Though many of the buildings captured in the earlier aerial views still stand today, you may not recognize them because their context has changed, and they no longer dwarf their neighbors.

I have arranged the images in the book in chronological order, to provide a sweeping historical view of the many iterations of Midtown and Uptown Manhattan over the years. As you turn the pages, note the subtle differences from year to year as the city continued to grow and change. Due to the high quality of most these photographs, many pages include a zoomed-in version of the original photograph, showing some details of interest.

1888: A bird's-eye view looking north along Fifth Avenue from 52nd Street. At this time, church steeples were the tallest points in the city. Note the Dakota apartment building on Central Park West at 72nd Street, which had been completed in 1881.

c. 1900: This image highlights the Washington Bridge over the Harlem River, connecting Manhattan and the Bronx at 181st Street. Built in 1889, this steel arch was one of the city's early bridge engineering masterpieces.

1902, 1904: Herald Square is wholly unrecognizable in these two stereoscope images. Both images are looking north at the junction of Broadway and Sixth Avenue with the Herald Building (low rise at the junction of the two roads) and the elevated railway. The Herald Building, located at 36th Street and headquarters for one of New York's famous newspapers of the time (and for which the Square was named), was demolished in 1921.

1905, 1907: At top, workers on the Times Building standing precariously (and seemingly fearlessly) 350 feet above the street. Though this stereoscope image is copyrighted 1905, it must have been taken the year before, since construction was already complete by 1905. The bottom image is looking north along Broadway and Seventh Avenue from the top of the recently completed Times Building. The Astor Hotel at 44th-45th Streets is at left. It opened in 1904 and the building was there until 1967, when it was demolished to make way for a skyscraper, the 54-story One Astor Plaza. Note the numerous streetcars.

1908, 1915: At top, a view from workers on the Metropolitan Life tower looking down on neighboring Madison Square. At bottom, looking down on the Flatiron Building from the completed, much taller Metropolitan Life Building. In the early days of the twentieth century, great achievements in building height were made in just a few years. As of 1908, the tallest building in the world was the Park Row Building in lower Manhattan at 390 feet. By 1909, the new leader was the Met Life Building at 700 feet.

c. 1912: At top, looking north along Broadway and Fifth Avenue from south of 23rd Street. The Broadway skyscraper in the distance is the Times Building at 42nd Street. At least nine streetcars can be seen along Broadway in this image. Below, the second iteration of Madison Square Garden at 26th Street, which was in use until 1926. After that, the Garden moved away from Madison Square but retained its place-specific name, which had nothing to do with its shape, which is today round.

ABOVE

5/1916: The Preparedness Parade moving up Fifth Avenue past the New York Public Library. The Preparedness Movement was a campaign that was aimed toward improving America's military strength and getting its citizens ready for the inevitability of a coming war.

BELOW

1916: Columbia University relocated from its longtime Midtown home to a new location in Morningside Heights in 1897. At the time, it must have seemed like practically the suburbs because it was so far removed from the bustle of the city center. However, it was easily accessible from Midtown starting in 1904, when the 116th Street subway station opened, one of the original stations in the system.

1918: A man known as the "Human Squirrel," who did many daring "stunts" in climbing for the benefit of World War I Relief Funds in New York City. He is shown here at a dizzy height in Times Square. The building in the background is the Times Building, aka One Times Square.

3/25/1919: Above, a rope stretches across the newly erected World War I Victory Arch at Madison Square just before an Honor Man of the 27th Division cut it to permit the parade to pass under it. There were great crowds on hand to watch the occasion. Below, the parade of the New York National Guard's 27th Division passing in front of the Court of the Honored Dead in a view taken from atop the New York Public Library on Fifth Avenue.

1919: The temporary Victory Arch at Madison Square as seen from the Met Building. The Great War, as it was called at the time, was the most expansive and frightening conflict America had ever known and its end in favor of the Allies was a tremendous relief; the victory and the war's veterans were celebrated.

9/10/1919: "The great checkerboard" of the city as seen from an airplane. The street plan of Midtown and Uptown looks far different from that of Lower Manhattan in that their streets were laid out according to the Randel Plan grid of 1811, as opposed to the earlier, more haphazard layout below 14th Street.

4/27/1925: This view of the Hell Gate Bridge was taken from Astoria, Queens. The heavily residential neighborhood in the foreground remains mostly the same, building-wise. Randalls Island and then Upper Manhattan (and beyond that, New Jersey) are visible in the distance.

7/4/1925: The Defense Day Parade seen from 1,000 feet up, marching past Grant's Tomb. The beautiful old building in the foreground is the Claremont Inn. Built in 1804 as a private home, it was once home to Joseph Bonaparte, Napoleon's brother and the former king of Spain. Once it was converted to an inn, it had many famous guests. In the 1930s it was a restaurant. It was torn down in 1951 and there is now a playground on the spot. Below is a view of the building in 1936, by which time it was already on the decline.

3/8/1928: Looking west from above Bryant Park. The lack of skyscrapers west of Eighth Avenue is very obvious. The Hudson River waterfront at far left is where the Jacob Javits Convention Center is located today. The Sixth Avenue Elevated railway line is visible in front of Bryant Park. This line was demolished in 1939 and replaced by the subway.

10/30/1928: Looking down on Manhattan from 6,000 feet up. Note the gap in skyscrapers between Lower Manhattan and Midtown Manhattan. This image predates the Empire State and Chrysler Buildings.

4/15/1931: Two views of navy blimps over Midtown, taken from 2,500 feet in altitude. People can be seen in the gondola at bottom. In more recent years, the Goodyear blimp was a sight that millions of New Yorkers saw in the sky during special events.

4/15/1931: Navy blimps over Midtown. The Empire State and Chrysler Buildings had only recently been completed when this photograph was taken from an altitude of 2,500 feet.

5/1931: Another view from 23,000 feet up, looking south from high above Upper Manhattan. From such a height it is hard to distinguish very many landmarks other than the largest, such as Central Park and the George Washington Bridge. Grant's Tomb and the Riverside Church can be made out upon enlargement. Note the ten Harlem River bridges in this image.

5/1931: From 23,000 feet up, Manhattan looks like a diorama. One striking thing to note is how the dense cluster of wharves along the Hudson River suddenly comes to an end around 59th Street—yet notice the extensive wharves and docks across the river in New Jersey. The George Washington Bridge was, and still is, the only Manhattan bridge crossing over the Hudson River (there are two tunnels: Lincoln and Holland).

1931, 1932: Two views looking northeast from the top of the Empire State Building. The views are almost identical, but there are two noticeable differences: the building behind the Chrysler Building is still under construction in 1931, and is completed in the bottom photo, as is another building to the left foreground. New York was then and is still ever-changing, with construction on new skyscrapers ongoing.

6/1932: A great and rare look down on the Empire State Building, only a year after it opened. The details of the pre-television antenna top can be clearly seen in this photograph, as can some of the Art Deco flourishes below the 102nd floor observation deck. The cars and people on the street and sidewalk below are surprisingly clear.

7/11/1932: The Hell Gate Bridge, seen from 700 feet up, was completed in 1916. This attractive steel arch rail bridge connects Randalls Island with Queens. The Empire State Building and the Manhattan skyline are visible in the distance, as is what was then known as Welfare Island but is now called Roosevelt Island. Hell Gate is where the steamship General Slocum caught fire and burned in 1904, killing over 1,000 people.

4/6/1935: This photograph captures the Army Day Parade along 5th Avenue from 1,500 feet up. It also highlights the massive size of the Central Park Lake. It also captures the northern edge of the Metropolitan Museum of Art complex.

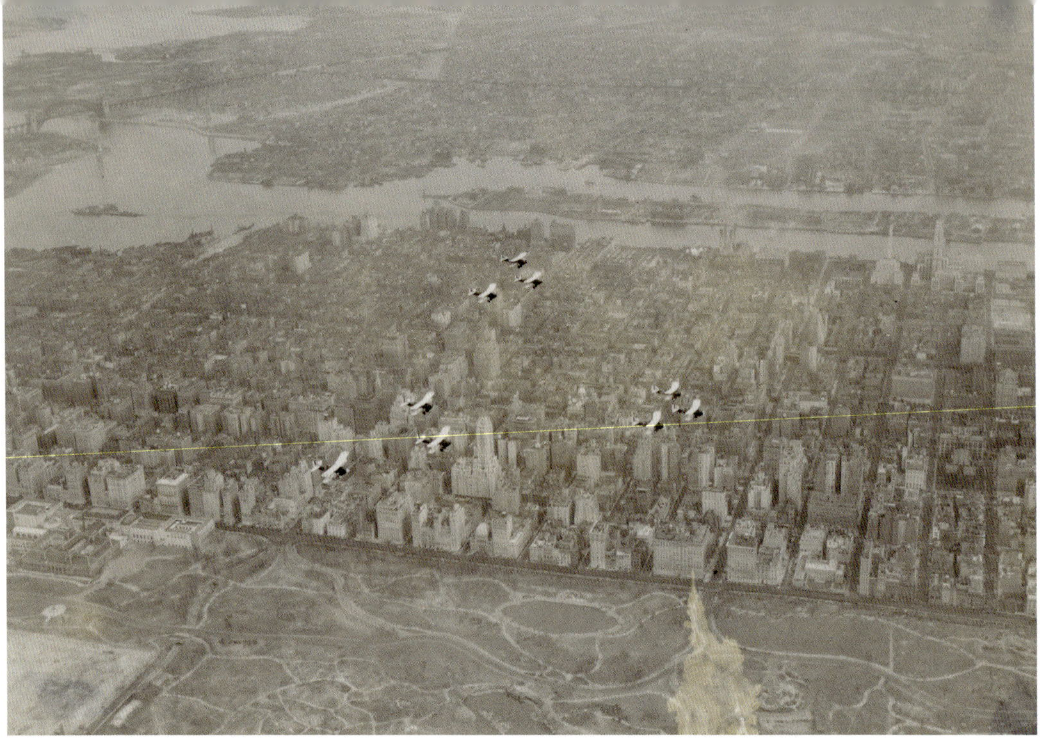

ABOVE

4/6/1935: In this photograph taken from 3,000 feet up, airplanes of the 9th Group are flying over Central Park for the Army Day Parade. The parade featured 15,000 men marching. It was the seventh consecutive year the parade was held in New York City.

BELOW

9/30/1935: A straight-on view of the George Washington Bridge and Upper Manhattan from 1,000 feet in altitude. What a strange thing it must have been in the early 1930s when the quiet uptown neighborhood was transformed by the construction of this massive bridge and its extensive approach ramps.

12/17/1935: The land along Central Park quickly became valuable once the park was built in the mid-nineteenth century. By the 1930s, apartment buildings, office buildings, and hotels ran along the south, east, and west sides of the park. The northern edge, however, was relatively underdeveloped.

12/17/1935: A great view of the Hudson Train Yards. The elevated railroad line that curves around to parallel the river is now the High Line. The Hudson Yards is now home to the Vessel and the Shed, as well as the 1,287-foot-high 30 Hudson Yards building, which features the Edge observation deck. In the distance are the Empire State Building and the Chrysler Building.

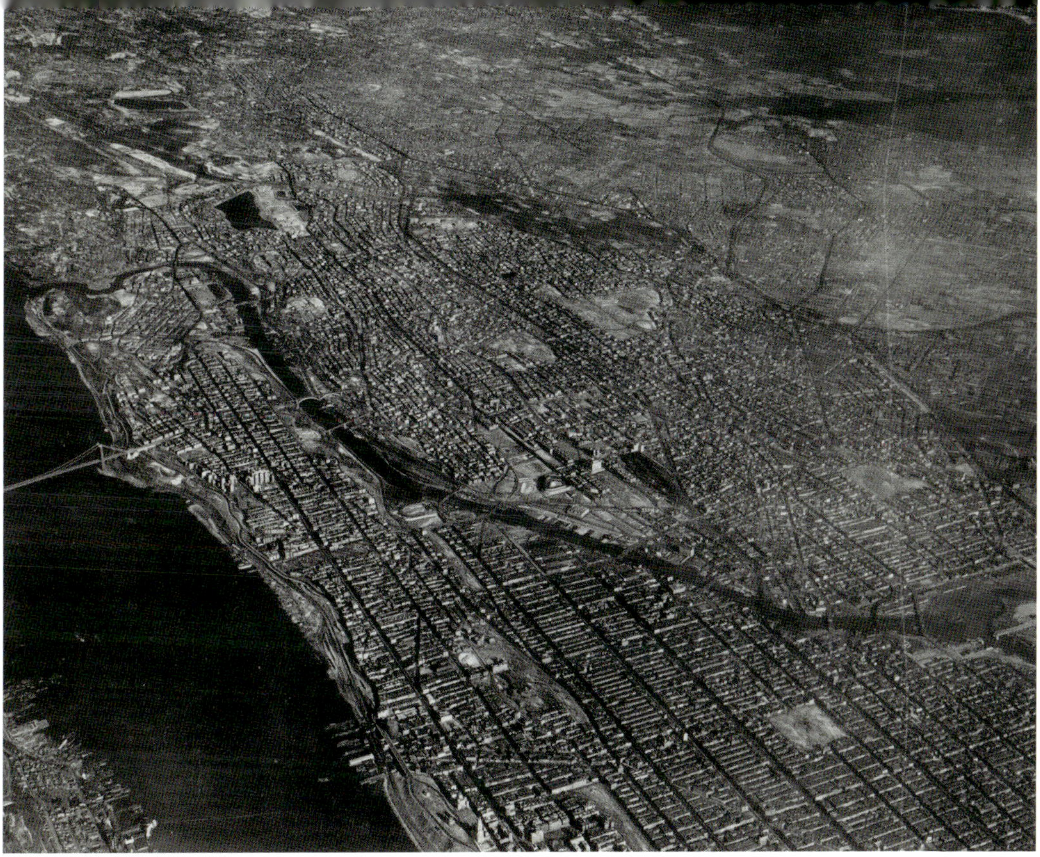

12/23/1935: Upper Manhattan and the Bronx from an altitude of 16,000 feet. What is especially evident in this image is the uniformity in height and size of block after block of buildings in Upper Manhattan. The proximity of Yankee Stadium to the Polo Grounds is obvious in this image.

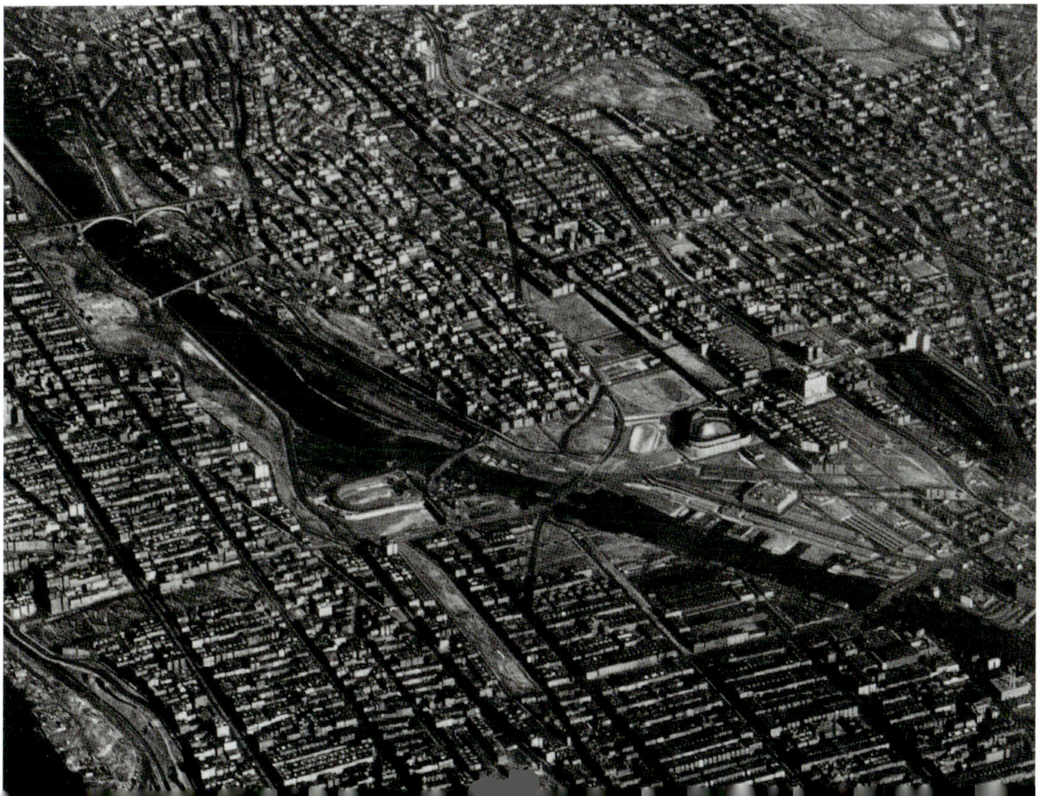

2/3/1936: Rockefeller Center from 1,700 feet up. St. Patrick's Cathedral, for decades the tallest structure by far in the entire area, is now dwarfed by the buildings of the complex, as are all the other surrounding buildings.

6/29/1936: A view of the 79th Street Rotunda/Boat Basin and the Henry Hudson Parkway (Route 9A) both under construction in this photograph that shows 76th through 83rd Streets. Also visible is Riverside Park, this section of which was still under construction as well. Riverside Drive is in the background.

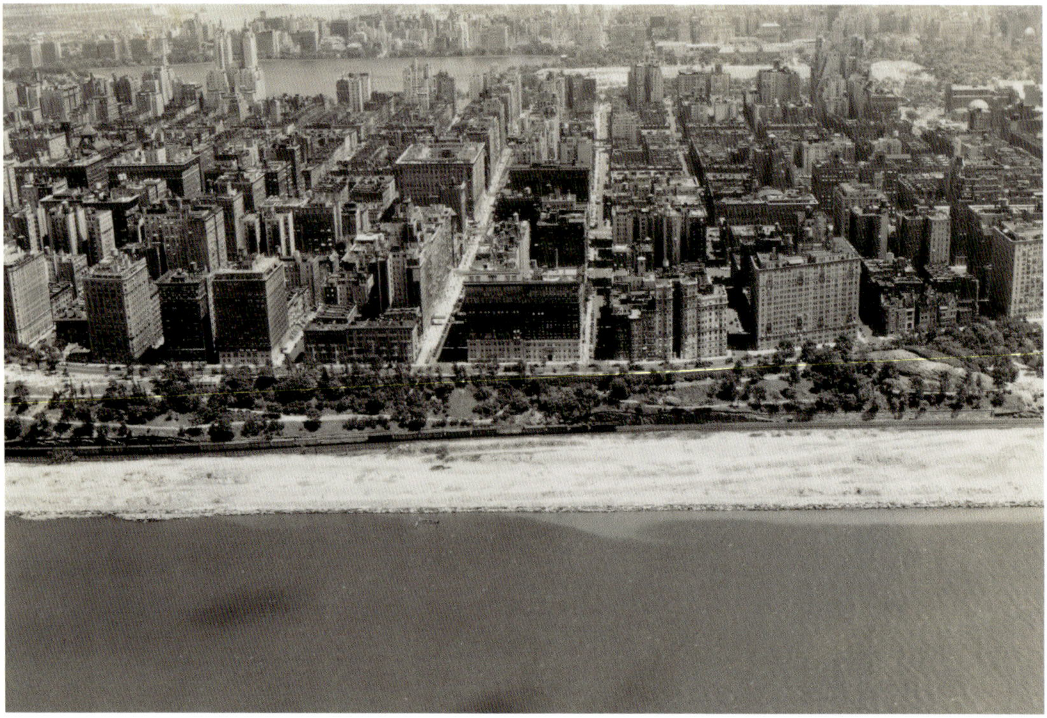

6/29/1936: The west side of Manhattan from 82nd to 89th Streets from 800 feet up. The drop-off from Riverside Drive is steep. The Henry Hudson Parkway (Route 9A) has yet to be built. Note the freight train on the tracks along the river. The Central Park Lake is visible in the distance.

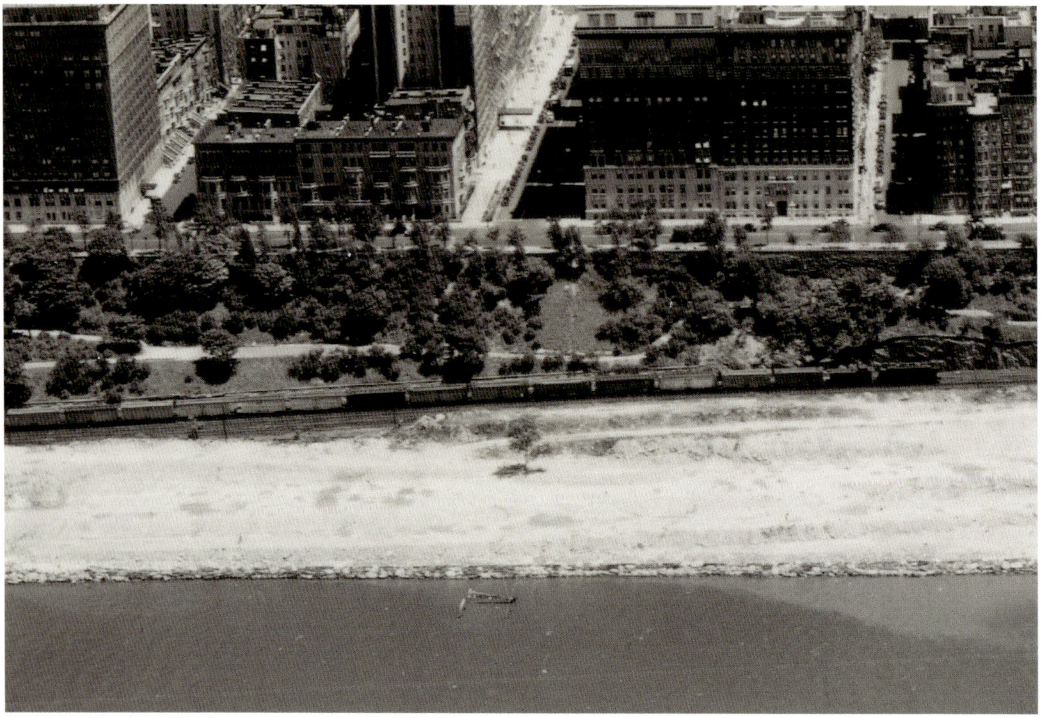

6/29/1936: Riverside Drive from 93rd to 99th Streets from 500 feet up. Note the construction equipment along the waterfront. There are numerous ten-to-twenty-story apartment buildings in the blocks closest to the river. Central Park is in the distance.

6/29/1936: Riverside Drive from 100th to 108th Street from 600 feet up. In the foreground, some older brownstones remain amongst newer, taller apartment buildings. In the distance, the Hell Gate Bridge (left, built 1916) and the recently completed and soon-to-open Triborough Bridge (now called the Robert F. Kennedy Bridge, it was opened in July of 1936).

0768-876A-8(6-29-36-12:47P)(12-800)   TIEMAN PL. TO 122 ST. RIVERSIDE DR., N.Y.C.

6/29/1936: The West Side of Manhattan from 122nd Street to Tieman Place from 800 feet. Two landmarks in this image are Grant's Tomb and the Riverside Church (opened in 1930). At 392 feet high, the church towers over all its neighbors in this image.

6/29/1936: Looking east toward 30 Rock from an altitude of 700 feet, it's clear how slender the building is. Note the numerous four-story apartment buildings on 51st and 52nd Streets between Fifth and Sixth Avenues. The approach to the 59th Street Bridge is at top left.

ABOVE

12/8/1936: For years, there were no buildings near the Empire State Building (aside from the Chrysler Building) that were anywhere close to its height, allowing aerial views to capture much of its Art Deco lower stories, too. The second tallest structure in this image is 30 Rock, fourteen blocks to the north. The 700-foot-high MetLife Building's peak (Madison Square) is in the foreground. The photograph was taken from an altitude of only 1,000 feet.

BELOW

1936: The hulking mass of Presbyterian Hospital at 168th Street and Broadway had been recently constructed (1928) when this photograph was taken. As of 2021 it is known as NewYork-Presbyterian Columbia University Irving Medical Center.

12/8/1936: The East River waterfront in the 40s, before the United Nations complex was built, was fairly industrial and not entirely attractive. Note the advertisement on the building for Wilson & Co. selling hams, bacon, and lard. The reclamation of Manhattan's waterfront was a process that began with the United Nations and continues to this day with such improvements as the "creation" of South Street Seaport and the opening of the Hudson River Greenway.

12/8/1936: Looking across the top of the 59th Street Bridge at midtown. At far left is the 30 Rock building. Gas tanks at 61st and 62nd Streets and an industrial presence along the waterfront are definite signs that this area was not as gentrified as it is today.

12/8/1936: Looking north toward the 59th Street Bridge, aka Queensboro Bridge, aka Ed Koch Queensboro Bridge. The bridge was completed in 1909 and offered the first bridge connection between Manhattan and Queens. At the time, the island it crossed over was known as Welfare Island; today it is Roosevelt Island. That is York Avenue at left running north-south under the bridge approach. The FDR Drive has not yet been started at this location; the only section complete by this point was near the Triborough Bridge.

2/11/1937: A view from 3,000 feet up looking northwest from the East River, toward midtown. Hoboken, New Jersey is visible at left, and beyond that, the marshland which currently houses MetLife Stadium, home of the Giants and Jets football teams.

1937: The recently completed 850-foot-high Art Deco 30 Rockefeller Plaza building (1933) is the star of this aerial photograph and was among the tallest buildings in the city when it was built. At bottom, note the Essex House sign; the forty-four-story building was built in 1931 as a luxury hotel (also in the Art Deco style). As of 2021 it was known as the JW Marriott Essex House.

10/27/1937: Looking at the south side of the Empire State Building from 2,050 feet up.

3/8/1938: This crisp image taken from 900 feet up shows Yankee Stadium in the foreground, and across the river in Manhattan, the oddly shaped Polo Grounds, home of the New York Giants. The Polo Grounds is long gone, and the original Yankee Stadium was replaced with a newer version in 2009.

1930s: This view, looking north from the Hudson River, shows several ships docked on Hudson piers, and the extensive wharf infrastructure that existed during the first half of the twentieth century.

2/8/1938: When this photograph was taken from 1,000 feet up, the George Washington Bridge had been open for less than six years. What is notable is the incredibly light traffic for 11:45 am. Most of the five-story apartment buildings in the image are still extant.

7/21/1938: Two night views of the Henry Hudson Parkway looking north from the top of 50 Riverside Drive (built 1930). The circular structure is the 79th Street Rotunda or traffic circle. New then, as of 2021 the structure was undergoing a major restoration.

3/11/1940: Looking east from over the Hudson River at midtown Manhattan from an altitude of 1,300 feet. Note the marked drop-off in the height of buildings just west of the Empire State Building. At bottom, the uniformity of the low-rise building rooftops is obvious.

3/11/1940: Looking east from over the Hudson River at the Upper West Side and Central Park. At bottom, note the advertisement for Ruppert Beer. Jacob Ruppert was a noted New York brewer whose beer brand outlasted him by a quarter of a century; he died in 1939 and the brewery, located on the East Side at 90th Street, closed in 1965. Ruppert was also the owner of the Yankees, responsible for buying Babe Ruth's contract from the Red Sox.

3/11/1940: A good view of the original Pennsylvania Station in this photograph taken from an altitude of 1,500 feet. The very architecturally similar post office building in the foreground was remade as the new Moynihan Train Hall, which opened in 2021 to rave reviews.

3/11/1940: Looking north at midtown Manhattan. The George Washington Bridge is visible in the distance at left and the 59th Street Bridge at right. This image gives a good view of what the East River shoreline was like before the United Nations was built.

3/11/1940: A great shot of the George Washington Bridge. At this point, the highway infrastructure that currently exists just across the Hudson River in Fort Lee, New Jersey, was simply non-existent. The way the bridge approach was hewn out of the Palisades cliffs is evident. On the Manhattan side, the Cloisters is visible in the cropped image below.

3/11/1940: This image shows the three most famous luxury transatlantic ocean liners of the time docked on the Hudson River. From left to right: *The Queen Elizabeth*, *Queen Mary*, and *Normandie*. For scale, notice the size of the cars on Route 9A in comparison to the massive ships. Less than two years after this photograph was taken, the *Normandie* burned and sank at this pier (Pier 88 at 48th Street).

3/26/1940: The Columbia University campus as seen from 2,000 feet. Originally located in Lower Manhattan, Columbia moved to 49th Street and Madison Avenue in 1857. In 1897, it moved to its current uptown location between 114th and 120th Streets on the west side. One of the architectural highlights of the campus is the domed Low Memorial Library, designed by Charles McKim of the famous firm McKim, Mead, and White.

3/26/1940: Times Square and environs from 2,000 feet up. In the left foreground is the stepped Paramount Building, which included the Paramount Theater, where Frank Sinatra and the Beatles would perform. On the next block is the Astor Hotel, and beyond that some old theaters which were demolished in the early 1980s (to the dismay of preservationists) to make room for the Marriott Marquis Hotel. When this photograph was taken, there were numerous hotels in the area, including the Paramount Hotel and the Hotel Edison.

1945: Looking south from the RCA Building (today's 30 Rock) at the Empire State Building. At that point, the ESB towered impressively over its nearest neighbors to its north, south, and west. Its biggest competition was the Chrysler Building (not in this image) to its northeast.

1/20/1949: The future site of the United Nations complex is notable in these images. By this point, the site had been cleared and construction was soon to start. The part of the FDR Drive through 59th Street had been completed.

8/1952: Broadway looking north from 165th Street. At the upper center of the image (169th Street), Broadway veers to the left and ends its boulevard nature. Trees still line the median along Broadway. The trees at right center are Mitchel Square, a city park named after Mayor John Purroy Mitchel, who died in World War I. Note the ad for Beacon floor wax. At bottom, Broadway looking north from just south of 173rd Street. Broadway is at left; the right part of the fork is Wadsworth Avenue, which continued north to 192nd Street. The church at right is the Fort Washington Presbyterian Church, built 1913.

8/1952: At top, Broadway looking south from 212th Street. The Cloisters is in visible on the hill in the distance. Note the trolley tracks running along Broadway. Just nine blocks north from here is the Broadway Bridge, which crosses the Harlem River to the Bronx. Left, Broadway south from 178th Street. Many of the buildings in the photo are still standing.

8/1952: The intersection of Broadway and Seventh Avenues looking north from 42d Street. The Times Building, once one of the tallest in the city, is in the foreground. The building is now unrecognizable, covered in cladding that allows giant billboards to be mounted on it at great profit. As of 2021, there is a Walgreens occupying the first few floors of the iconic building (from whence the New Year's ball drops). The Paramount Building is at left, towering above the nearby buildings; now it is dwarfed by its neighbors 1515 Broadway and the Marriott Marquis Hotel.

8/1952: Looking north from the intersection of Fifth Avenue and Broadway at 23rd Street. The Empire State Building looms large. Madison Square Park is at right. The A. C. Gilbert Company was famous for inventing the Erector Set, a favorite of generations of kids of all ages. The company went out of business in 1967, but Erector Sets continued to be made by Gabriel Industries.

ABOVE

8/1952: Broadway looking south from 108th Street. West End Avenue is on the right. In the triangle is the Straus Park Memorial at 106th Street. In the park is a memorial statue for Ida and Isidor Straus, who died on the *Titanic* in 1912.

BELOW

8/1952: Broadway south from Riverside Drive. In the foreground is the entrance to Fort Tryon Park, which opened in 1935 on land that had been gifted to the city by John D. Rockefeller. The Cloisters of the Metropolitan Museum of Art is visible at top right.

9/1952: Broadway looking south from 72nd Street. Knickerbocker Beer was a famous brand that was produced in New York City. The brewery at 92nd Street was in business through the 1960s. The small structure in the foreground at left is the 72nd Street subway entrance. It is still there today, but the building's appearance has been modernized.

Broadway looking north from 78th Street. On the corner of 79th Street, note the Woolworth's, once a common discount store in many locations around New York City. The last Woolworth's closed in 1997.

10/1952: Looking north from just south of Grant's Tomb. In this image, Henry Hudson Parkway is completed; compare this to the image on page 32 when it had not been constructed yet. At bottom, a view of the Columbia University campus, a few blocks southeast of Grant's Tomb.

11/1953, 12/1953: Above, Times Square at night. The Paramount Theater is at left in the foreground. *Calamity Jane* starring Doris Day and Howard Keel is playing there. The Hotel Astor is the next building at left. Below, the Empire State Building at night. The television tower we are so accustomed to had only been recently installed when this photo was taken. There is something romantic about the city at night in black and white, each building's lit windows a grid of light.

 At top, looking east from 41st Street towards Bryant Park and the New York Public Library. At bottom, looking west-northwest from Fifth Avenue and 40th Street at the library and Bryant Park. Though the park's fountain and great lawn are still recognizable, the dense forest-like tree cover that is evident in these photos no longer exists; the park has been remade as a more pedestrian friendly space. Beyond the park is Sixth Avenue. The stepped building in the distance is the Paramount Building (1926) on Broadway between 43rd and 44th Streets.

8/1958: Two contiguous views of Park Avenue looking south from over Grand Central Station (42nd Street). The roof of Grand Central is visible in both images. At top, the fifty-three-story One Grand Central Place, the forty-eight-story Mercantile Building, and the Empire State Building are visible to the right. One Grand Central Place and the thirty-six-story 100 Park Avenue visible to the right at bottom.

7/1959: The United Nations complex covers 18 acres and consists of four main buildings: the Secretariat, the General Assembly, Conference Area (including Council Chambers) and the Library. Construction began in 1949 and cost $65 million. The General Assembly first met in this Hall at the opening of its seventh regular annual session, on 14 October 1952. At bottom, a *circa* late 1950s or early 1960s view of the complex.

1964: A striking view looking north at the Pan Am Building (now the MetLife Building or 200 Park Avenue) and the Chrysler Building. The 1950s and 60s generation of skyscrapers was far different looking than their Art Deco and Classical predecessors of the 1900-1940s era. Straighter lines, more geometric, often rectangular shapes set these buildings apart.

5/1973: Two views of the Manhattan approaches to the George Washington Bridge. Both views are looking south with the bridge entrance to the right, from slightly different perspectives. The Henry Hudson Parkway crosses under the bridge approach and has looping ramps leading to and from the bridge. The main bridge approach is I-95, aka the Cross Bronx Expressway.

6/1974: Untreated sewage flowing into the East River at 79th Street and the FDR Drive as part of a series of photographs taken by the Environmental Protection Agency to document pollution in New York City.

c. 1976: Upper Manhattan and the approach to the George Washington Bridge are seen in this 1970s photograph. Just left of the high-rise apartment buildings is the post-modern Greyhound George Washington Bridge Bus Station, which was designed by Pier Luigi Nervi and opened in 1963.

c. 1980s: Looking south at the Empire State Building. The top of the building was first lit in colors in 1976; to celebrate the bicentennial it was lit in red, white, and blue. The color display has since grown more sophisticated, using a state-of-the-art LED lighting system, capable of displaying more than 16-million colors. The Twin Towers are in the distance.

1980s: Times Square at night in an image that dates to the reign of the Broadway musical 42nd Street, which opened in 1980 and closed in 1989. Times Square in the 1980s had become seedy and dangerous; it was only in the 1990s that it was cleaned up and began its rejuvenation as a proper tourist destination.

c. 1990s: This view looks east from Eleventh Avenue toward the Hudson Yards before they were today's Hudson Yards, partly covered over and developed with the Vessel and skyscrapers. Tenth Avenue crosses over the train yard. The future High Line is the green-covered strip that curves around and then runs parallel to the train yard tracks.

10/1996: Two views from the 22nd floor of One Penn Plaza, looking west and south. The round structure in the foreground is the roof of Madison Square Garden. The Twin Towers are visible in the distance.

4/11/2002: Satellite imagery looking down on Manhattan. At top, Midtown, part of Central Park, and the Upper West Side. At bottom, the East Side; the United Nations is visible at top along the East River—to the right are Queens and Brooklyn separated by Newtown Creek and spanned by the Kosciusko Bridge.

5/22/2002: Some of the Naval warships that participated in Fleet Week 2002, docked at Pier 88 next to the Aircraft Carrier USS *Intrepid*, which was converted into a Sea-Air-Space Museum. Some of the visible ships include the Destroyer USS *Edson* (right, in front of the *Intrepid*), the Guided Missile Frigate USS *Elrod* (foreground) and the Royal Danish Navy Ocean Patrol Vessel HDMS *Thetis*. Bottom: The Destroyer USS *Peterson* sails up the Hudson River, as her crew prepares to join in the festivities of Fleet Week 2002. More than 6,000 Sailors, Marines, and Coast Guard personnel aboard twenty-two ships sailed into New York City for the 15th Annual Fleet Week in 2002.

ABOVE

9/24/2003: US Air Force F-16 CJ Fighting Falcon, 20th Fighter Wing wing ship from Shaw Air Force Base, South Carolina, flying over New York City during a North American Aerospace Defense (NORAD) Operation mission. The Falcon is armed with AIM-120C Advanced Medium Range Air-to-Air Missile and AIM-9M Sidewinder missiles and equipped with 370-gal fuel tanks. Central Park is visible below the aircraft.

BELOW

9/24/2003: US Air Force F-16 CJ Fighting Falcon, 20th Fighter Wing wing ship from Shaw Air Force Base, South Carolina, wing ship refuels from a USAF KC-135R Stratotanker, 319th Air Refueling Wing, Grand Forks AFB, North Dakota, during a NORAD Operation over New York City.

8/27/2013: Looking north, a view of Central Park South from the Top of the Rock. At bottom, turning south, a perspective of the Empire State Building can be had that is unlike any other available view of the iconic skyscraper.

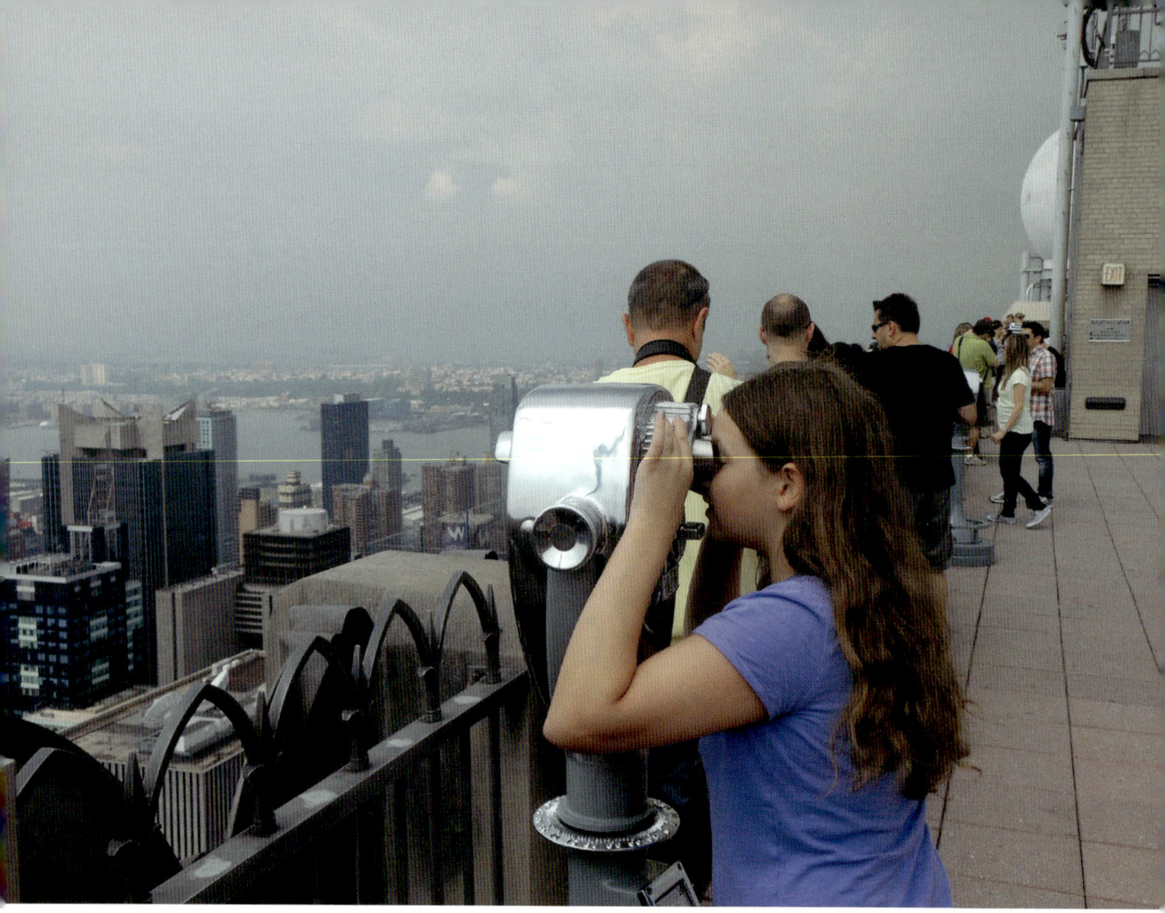

8/27/2013: The Top of the Rock observation deck 850 feet atop 30 Rockefeller Plaza offers a great vantage point in all directions. The open deck is unique in its position literally atop the flat roofed building.

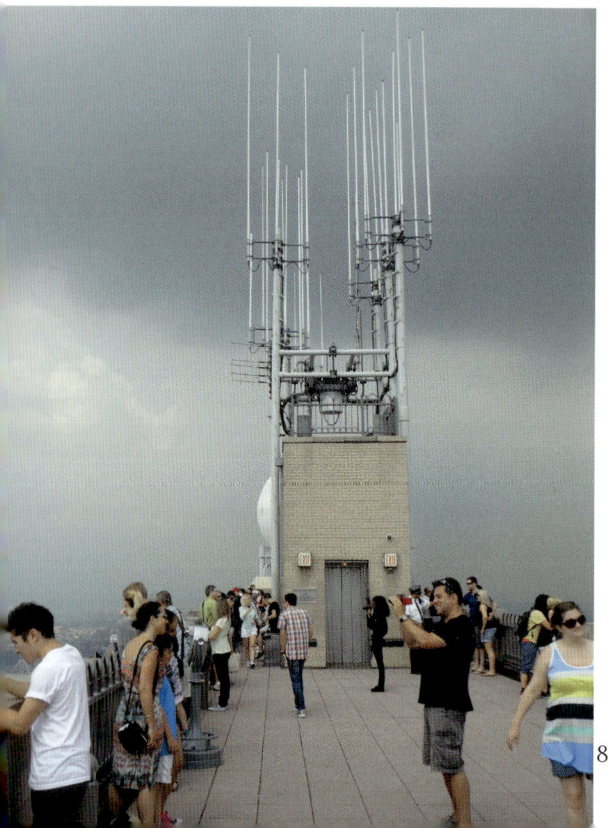

9/28/2015: Looking northeast from the eighty-sixth-floor observation deck on the Empire State Building. The United Nations building is at far right. The skyscrapers of Long Island City are in the background. Note several residential towers in the eastern part of midtown. At bottom, a view looking northwest. The skyscraper in the foreground at left is the 1,200-foot-high Bank of America Tower, the eighth tallest building in New York City as of 2021.

9/28/2015: No matter how many new skyscrapers are built in midtown, the Chrysler Building will always be a standout. The shimmering, elegant Art Deco stylings of the top of the tower are eye-catching from any angle. The radiating semi-circles are like crowns to adorn this building which was briefly the tallest in the world until it was surpassed by the Empire State Building, from whence this photograph was taken.

9/28/2015: Looking north from the Empire State Building toward 432 Park Avenue, a slender condominium tower that was completed three months after this photograph was taken. At 1,396 feet high, the building was second tallest in the city when finished, but by 2021 had fallen to fifth on the list due to the completion of One Vanderbilt, 111 West 57th Street, and the Central Park Tower. At bottom, looking west from the ESB toward the Hudson River. The tower at right is the 1,046-foot-high New York Times Building on Eighth Avenue, completed in 2007. The slender black building at center is the vintage 1970s One Penn Plaza, which as of 2021 was being remodeled and called Penn 1.

9/18/2015: Looking east from the eighty-sixth-floor observation deck on the Empire State Building. No longer even among the top five tallest buildings in Manhattan, the Empire State is still nonetheless the most popular and iconic skyscraper tourist attraction. At bottom, looking east-north-east from the enclosed 102nd-floor observation deck. The United Nations is visible just right of the shadow cast by the Empire State Building.

12/30/2015: Looking down at the first floor of the iconic Guggenheim Museum (5th Avenue and 89th Street) from an upper floor, one of the more interesting indoor "aerial" views to be had in the city. The building was designed by Frank Lloyd Wright.

6/2/2016: Looking south from about 30th Street toward the 700-foot-high Met Life Tower, built 1909 between 23rd and 24th Streets. In many parts of Midtown and Uptown Manhattan, even mid-rise buildings offer decent views of the skyline.

OPPOSITE PAGE

5/18/2017: On this sunny spring day in 2017, a man drove his car on a path of destruction, heading onto the sidewalk at a high speed in Times Square from 42nd to 45th Street, killing one and injuring twenty-two people before smashing into a bollard. Since this incident, numerous bollards have been erected to prevent something similar from happening again. Looking north along Broadway at 44th Street just after the incident, a piece of the car can be seen.

8/21/2017: Two views of the crowd gathered in Times Square, looking up to see the solar eclipse. At top, 2:31 pm, and bottom, 2:39 pm. The eclipse peaked in New York City at 2:44 pm.

ABOVE
1/26/2018: Looking west from the Empire State Building at the several skyscrapers that were under construction at the time. What was once the relatively dilapidated Hudson Yards/Chelsea/Hell's Kitchen neighborhoods have seen tremendous growth in the twenty-first century.

BELOW
1/26/2018: Looking north from the Empire State Building at dusk. The 1,396-foot-high 432 Park Avenue residential tower is visible at right.

4/27/2018: At top, looking north along Second Avenue from the Roosevelt Island Tram at 59th Street. At bottom, looking south along the waterfront of Manhattan from the tram at the top of the Ed Koch Queensboro Bridge, aka 59th Street Bridge.

1/24/2019: A couple of rainy views looking north on upper Times Square from the eighth floor of the Marriott Marquis Hotel. The images were taken only a couple of minutes apart; the changing digital billboard advertisements change the entire color scheme and aesthetic of the view instantly.

6/9/2021: This image taken from the nearby GE Building highlights two famous old Central Park-facing hotels: the Sherry-Netherland Hotel at 781 Fifth Avenue, and the Pierre Hotel at 2 East 61st Street.

6/10/2021: Above, Looking north along Tenth Avenue from the High Line. Below, looking east along 18th Street from just west of 10th Avenue from the High Line. This public walkway offers great elevated views of Chelsea. It was created from an old elevated rail line that had been long since abandoned. An eyesore was transformed into a magical place, a 1.45-mile park and trail with great views and plenty of flowering plants.

6/10/2021: At top, looking east along 23rd Street from just west of Tenth Avenue from the High Line. At bottom, 20th Street looking east from just west of Tenth Avenue from the High Line. The old brick building on the corner is the High Line Hotel, which was once a dormitory (built 1895) for an Episcopal seminary. The land was once owned by Clement Clarke Moore, author of the famous Christmas poem, who donated it to the Episcopal Church.

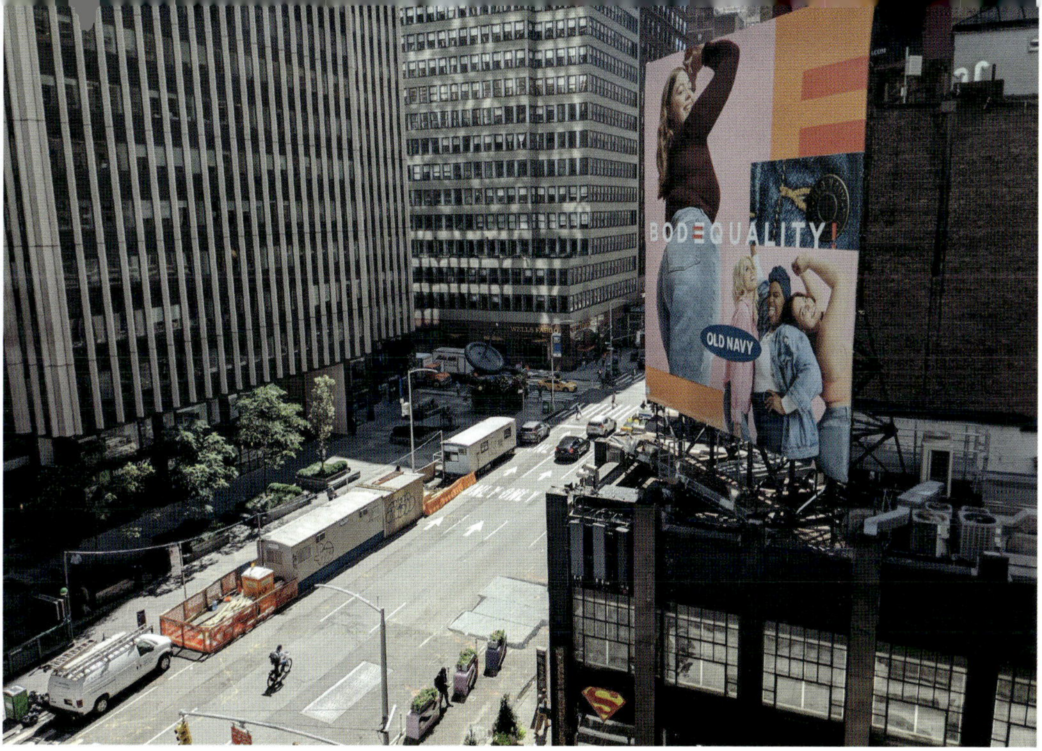

Above
9/2/2021: Looking south on Seventh Avenue from 40th Street. The popular Midtown Comics store is in the building on the corner in the foreground.

Below
9/2/2021: Looking north on Seventh Avenue from 47th Street, the northern end of Times Square. A tiny bit of Central Park's greenery is visible in the far distance.

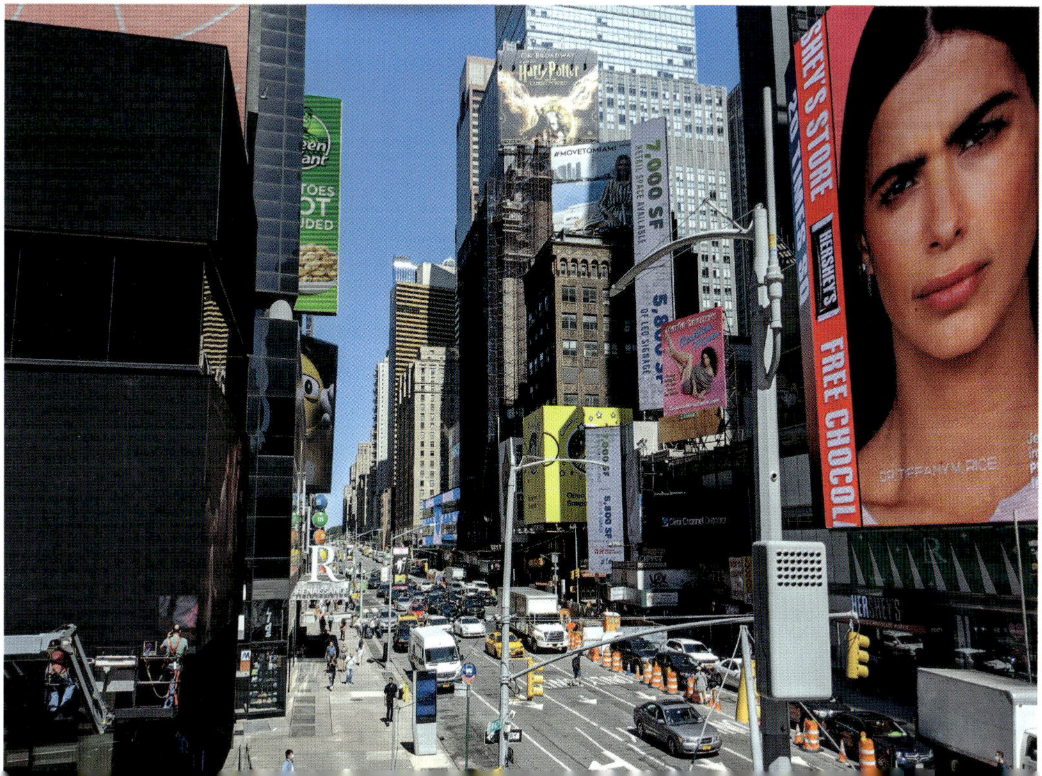

ABOVE
9/2/2021: Looking at the Time Square Wheel, a 110-foot-high Ferris wheel that was temporarily installed at 47th Street and Broadway in the summer of 2021.

BELOW
9/7/2021: A view of 34th Street looking west from Seventh Avenue from the ninth floor of the Macy's department store. The building across the street is 450 Seventh Avenue, aka the Nelson Tower, a 560-foot-tall building built in 1931.